4:00 A.M.
A Productivity Argument

AUGUSTO PINAUD

Cover Design by: Isabel Pinaud

IsabelPinaudO@gmail.com

To those that insist in defy and disbelieve in the validity of:

"The Book of Normal".

CONTENTS

OTHER BOOKS BY THE AUTHOR

Productivity (Spanish):
- 25 Consejos de Productividad
- No

Productivity (English):
- 25 Tips for Productivity
- No

Fiction (English):
- The Writer
- Putsch. A Hannah Fisher Thriller

1 CURRENT REALITY.THE LACK OF FOCUS.

We all played the game of being normal, we've all tried to met the rules of the "Book of Normal". Thomas Moore said: "The need to be normal is the predominant anxiety disorder in modern life."

We should be struck by people's inability to focus and concentrate on the stuff they do. It should impress us even more, really it should worry us, that we like many of the people we know, lack the ability to focus. The sad part is that we see it as normal, since we are all the same. The reality is that all of us have use the same shoes to walk, we all have tried to do more than what we should on a moment. We all have more commitments than what we are going to be able to fulfill in a lifetime. We simply try to do more and more, regardless how important or relevant things are. Many of us have become resigned to this new reality. This is simply the way to survive in the modern life.

The problem isn't that we have been there. The problem is that for so many that's their only reality, that state in which they can't concentrate or focus for a long period of time. For many is the daily normal to have two or three meetings at the same time, more than once a day. The daily normal is check email while on a conference call, often putting the phone on "mute" so we can talk to someone that just walked in our office. We suppose and assume that anything it is possible; at the end of the day we are doing it constantly.

Without a doubt, I am particularly impressed by how people lack the ability to focus. It is interesting that we spend hours taking measures to control our surroundings, projects and tasks, only to without effortlessly invent an unlimited number of things to sabotage it. We are constantly looking for solutions to get more time. We do a great amount of work to see how we have more quantity instead of more quality. Maybe we have our focus on the wrong place, on that of being normal.

We look for solutions to make another conference call, one more sale, one more thing to add to our list. We have all being there-I am not in any way innocent of this. In fact, that was the reason I want it to learn about productivity; I have been guilty many times. The problem is that this one more thing has created a lack in our ability of concentrate, the ability of focus on the task on hand. We begin to write an email and send a tweet, review what our friend said in Facebook, get a phone call, send a text to our wife, write two more lines on that email, talk to the person that came into our office, write two more lines and hit click on send. Once that's done, we discover we have no clue about the content of that email, no clue about what we said, but we consider it with little relevance. That's normal. We know that if the recipient hasn't understood or guessed the content, he will call back so we can explain it. Honestly, it isn't that people don't care, is it simply that it is a routine, something normal. As all this routine happens with the next email and the one after that, and the one after that; in many cases for more than 300 times. 300 per day, five days a week, in other words, more than 1,500 times. I still remember when people use to complain about 50 daily emails. After that we complaint on one hundred, more than two hundred and now, more than three hundred as they said, is normal.

In reality, the problem with this new "normal", we have stopped thinking. Who has time to think after three hundred emails? The reality is that the number of emails that we receive daily were sent by other normal people that also don't have a minute to think. We receive these emails, search things on the web and more. The reality is that the excess of emails as well as the quantity of information that we are consuming is not going to decrease, no now, not ever. (Just for the record I mean the quantity of the information what it is going to decrease, not the quality of that information.) This trend is only going to increase and no one it is going to stop it. It is important to found a way to manage the volume and at the same time find a way to process and think so we can regain our day to day perspective.

Each day we act based on chaos and we try to answer more quickly, with less knowledge in our hands, hoping that at the end of the day things don't explode in our hands. The time to think, reflect, concentrate and focus simply doesn't exist for the majority. In many cases people can't remember the last time they had time to think, reflect, concentrate or focus, nor that when they had time to do it. The reality is that even at weird moments that we can slow down we are so tired that we can't think. Many times the reason we don;t stop is because we are exhausted. Stop to think: Never!

Even when we are willing to deny this reality in which many are living, more of us are looking for ways to break with the current reality; some have decided simplify to the extreme, others used to a certain lifestyle and responsibilities that they have create, are looking to ways to manage the information that they receive, try to process and even look for an opportunity to think and find some perspective on their own life.

Many are desperately looking for solution, looking for something that help them do all those pending things, finish all those things they had compromise themselves, plus all those that are important for them. Somehow we want to accomplish everything and more. The reality is that we can do anything, but not everything, at least not at the same time.

2 LOOKING INTO PERSONAL IMPROVEMENT.

The reality is like I said: that I have been guilty of trying to survive the week on four hours of sleep per night, trying to wake up earlier and work as late as my brain allow it. Trying to do as many task as possibly, reply to most of my emails and provide as many solutions as possible.

The reality is that even, knowing that my work is less effective when I try to work more hours and sleep less, I simply didn't take that knowledge into consideration, because I felt that if I stopped, everything was going to run me over.

Like many, I was trying to gain as many hours as possible on the day, most efficient ways so my system allow me to do even more. In other words I was trying to do more of what taking me nowhere. You know, I was acting out as an insane person according to Albert Einstein: doing the same thing and hoping for a different result. Eventually the crisis and the collapse came. I simply could not handle anymore.

In crisis and without being effective at all, I tried to continue moving forward, do more than what I was able to, but I was getting more and more behind, more frustrated and more unhappy. I decided that things could not get much worse, so it was time to stop everything, sit down and imagine how I could make everything better and different—scratch everything and start again. In a way I declared Emotional Bankruptcy with everything and was hoping to find something different, different from what I was doing and wasn't giving me any results—what I assume now was giving me "normal" results.

The first step was get back to basics, get back and read those books that initiated me in the productivity game. Sometimes the best we can do is get a blank page and think. Get out of the panic state took me a little bit because everything was coming down and I maybe would not recover. The difference with this collapse is that I realized I needed to stop. It was forcing me to think. I was focused on looking for a solution. I was feeling great, it was like I found an old friend. From there I began to make a list of those tricks that over the years had help me before everything failed and began to rebuild everything little by little. Piece by piece.

My objective was to accomplish all my life's goals, continue evolving and growing. Therefore I decided continue looking for a solution, something that could help me get to my goal, that would allow me to share the life I was dreaming of with my wife and kids. The big questions were: to discover, What was missing? What I didn't had?

I wish I could say that I sat, brewed coffee and in the next fifteen minutes I found the answer. The reality is that I spend weeks writing, making mind-maps, writing more, looking where I had lost the way. I spent weeks thinking. Planning. Dreaming. Eventually, I got to the moment in which everything fit, in which everything make sense and finally said: Eureka!

I Finally understood that the problem wasn't the amount of things I had to do, not the incredible amount of information that I should consume, nor the lack of time. The problem was simpler: I had forgotten how to focus and concentrate so I could accomplish stuff. The only hours that I was using to think weren't enough. It wasn't that I had lost the way, it was that I had stopped thinking about which direction I should take for the next step. I was trying to see how I could control the information that was reaching my hands, digest it, process it and decided what to do—All this without taking a moment to think, the fastest the better. All this was creating something simple: paralysis.

I was trying to do so much at the same time that I wasn't effective at any of them, so I decided to stop and think for a moment.

The solution was simple: I needed time to concentrate, to think, to focus my efforts. Immediately I began to doubt this new conclusion—of course I don't have time. I had try to look for some in the middle of the day. At the end of the day and in many other ones. I had tries every hour possible; it was simply impossible. The problem is you can't deceive yourself. Considering the argument of being a night owl, there was a time that I had never tried before. 4:00 A.M.

3 THE 4:00 A.M. EXPERIMENT.

Before you have any doubt about this, the first time I though about waking up at 4:00 A.M., I think the nicest thing I said to myself was that I was crazy. (Honestly it was more colorful than that.)

I began convincing myself that I worked better at night, that I wasn't a morning person and even worse at 4:00 A.M. That it is not even the morning. Only crazy people wake up at that time. Who thinks about waking up at that time? (More than you and I believe if we need to ask that question.) At that time not even the dogs at home want to be up. I spent hours trying to convince myself that I was insane. That without a doubt it was going to be a waste of time. I had never been successful waking up earlier. For years I had joke that the connection between my brain and the rest of my body only happened after a lot of time had passed from the moment I had been up, so why I was going to waste that time instead of staying in bed and sleeping. But like many things I had discovered and that had make me productive, I had to try it and prove that was a waste of time. "Two weeks" I told myself and continue saying, "after two weeks this is over, because this idea is ridiculous and illogical."

The first week was exactly what I had thought. I had predicted how bad was going to be. I struggled waking up, it was a huge effort. After that I sit at my desk with a cup of coffee, without being really able to wake up, think or actually do anything. I was wasting time on the biggest way possible. It was something incredible. Now I was getting out of bed earlier. I could barely made it every night to the moment that everyone was getting to bed. I was exhausted and couldn't do anything else. I was doing even fewer things, I had fewer hours in the day—to top that I was wasting hours in the morning in which I could not think, or wake up or anything else. Everything around me was crumbling. Despite to the fact that my desperation and lack of patience were increasing, nothing was happening. Nothing except that everything was falling behind. I said two weeks, so I tried again the second week.

It was Wednesday of the second week, when finally I was able of accomplish the first useful thing, in silence. Finally, I had been able to cross something off of my list for the first time in the morning. I was feeling better, but I wasn't in any way productive. This is not even close to the level of productivity that I really needed or dreamt to having. After eight days it, was the first time that I was able to cross anything, so I celebrated. Thursday and Friday were the same. But there was a difference: maybe not the most important, not maybe the most important choice, but something had been done in a different way. Finally the two weeks passed, but instead of feel happy about it, as I originally thought I would had feel, I wasn't ready to let this test go. There was something different being formed. Somehow, the idea of thinking seemed possible again. Therefore I decided to try for another week. "Three weeks and I will abandon this absurd project," I told myself, but not with the same conviction I had two weeks earlier.

When I went to sleep that Sunday, I went to bed with the hope that Monday was going to be productive, as was the end of the previous week. The interesting thing is that it was like that. It was even more productive than the previous week. As the week progressed, I was looking forward to getting deeper into this space that I had discover.

When Saturday arrived, my body woke up at 6:00 A.M, rested like I haven't been in years. I simply decided: read. It was a fantastic moment. Honestly, I read like I had not done in years.

Obviously the test was extended another week, and one more, and one more. As I extended each test, the voice inside my head was less and less convincing, until I finally decided to stop calling it a test and I transformed into my new routine.

One of the most interesting things about this experience is that for the first time in my life I woke up full of energy, I wake up with will; I had not used the snooze button 100 times (something that I am sure my wife appreciated). I wen to bed with the illusion of the hour(s) of work in the next morning. Sometimes just to think, sometimes to do research, other times to write.

One of the most incredible things is the fact that once the first two minutes happen under the water on the shower, I am totally up and full of energy and ready for the adventure. I had never had this happen to me before. Apparently I wasn't a cousin of an owl as I believe for years, I was able to work earlier, before the rest of the world around me begin to move.

For years, like most of the people I knew, I tried to work late. I try to make those late hours special so they will provide me with an advantage that would allow me to move forward and make a difference. I tried to create routines, projects, and more things after ten at night when everyone else was sleeping. I had never considered that instead of that I could go to bed and wake up even earlier, I never contemplated that the best way to accomplish my goals could been wake up at 4:00 A.M.

I now have a natural sense of peace that it is hard to explain, but have time to think. I don't have the need to run, hurry or stress in any way. At 4:00 A.M., you know you have the chance to think, to evaluate and to finish all those things that you will not be able at some other time.

It is a time that has proven itself to help me find some of my greatest ideas, clarity and productivity. Not only that, but by 9:00 A.M. when the rest of the world is ready to interact with me, I have four or five hours of productive time.

Most of the time, it's less. At 7:30 A.M. I have the luxury to get my daughter ready and drive her to school, but even when there are less than four hours as I mentioned in the previous paragraph, the hours that I do have, most of the time, are more productive than the rest of the day. My day has already an important victory.

Of course, waking up at 4:00 A.M. to go to Facebook is a waste of time, but choose the task with the highest impact can change how the rest of the day will be.

4 THE HIGHEST IMPACT TASK.

Once I understood that this experiment could bring me something useful and valuable I began to see how could I use it better. The reality is that at this time of the day, the right decision will provide the equivalent of four or more hours of work on a regular schedule.

There is not enough time to find, I have said many times that our most valuable resource isn't time. Time is all we have? and we all have the same. Commonly we believe the opposite; otherwise we would not complaint about lack of time constantly. Concentration and focus are our most valuable resources, since not all of us or are able to get the same; and even when we do, it is never on abundance. I knew that finding focus and concentration at this time was the most important thing. Honestly, at the beginning not every decision was good. Sometimes because my own clumsiness, others times because I picked what I was in the mood for and not what I should have picked.

One of the most important things that I have learned as I progressed in this experiment is that basically at this time of the day, the important thing to do is the task of most impact, even if it is not the most important one.

Once you discover what you can do in that hour of silence, in solitary confinement, full of energy, with coffee on hand and an infinite universe of possibilities, you discover that you are like Peter Parker. You discover that with a great power, comes a great responsibility.

It isn't that this is a new time; it's simply that as the volume of information increases disproportionately, as it has been for years the first thing that we sacrifice is our ability to think. We don't do it consciously but we spend each day thinking less and less; we spend more time running, more time in stress and therefore more moments simply tired, even exhausted to the extreme.

Once I began using that hour constantly, as I had the problem choosing which task to do first. In all the lists of tasks that I had contained more tasks that I will likely be able to do in the next couple of years, so picking the correct one was a challenge, a challenge that change everything.

As my days progressed I also began to notice that what

my instinct was picking as the most important wasn't necessarily what I should be doing, not because they wasn't important or even critical. It was because I couldn't accomplished those without the key element of this special hour: the ability to think, focus and reflect.

It was then that I begin looking for the task of biggest impact, that I had defined as that one that required the most concentration and focus as well as the ability to think and reflect. These properties made it the appropriate time that would create a feeling of success the rest of the day.

A complex definition, without a doubt. But it had been incredible effective.

There are many people on the time management world that talk about important things. I even mention them in my book "25 Tips for Productivity" on the chapter about the daily list. The daily for me is important, key in many instances, but not always had the task of most impact; in general it contain the most important tasks. Assume for a moment that you can use one hour a week to think about this task of most impact. Imagine that you get the same hour every day of the week. Now the whole month.

This is exactly why it's important to choose the task with the most impact. Assuming that there are four weeks in a month, we are talking about twenty hours to think and reflect. When was the last time you had that luxury?

In general, since things move at an incredible speed in this modern world (and in case of any doubt, they are going to move even faster) we have lost the ability of protect our time to think. It is a luxury that we assume others have—other fortunate people that maybe don't have the problems that we have. From there we go into a vicious circle that will never fix anything.

Those that have that luxury, don't have our problems because they have a better job than yours, nor more income. The reason they have time to think doesn't have any relation with the position they hold, nor the amount of work they have. The reason is that they had learned to protect their time. Many think that their time it is impossible to protect their time, because their salary, position, and the kind of work they do; but sadly they are wrong—wrong because they are trying to be part of what I called normal.

We all know that person who goes and exercise every day, regardless what's happening. It is not that they have more discipline, or they a better than you; they just know to protect their time, always. Think and make the task with the highest impact necessary for you to complete, like it is for that people that go to the gym everyday. Something to protect and plan for.

5 A PRODUCTIVITY ARGUMENT

CONCLUSION.

For some reason that I don't understand yet, in general we structure our day in a way that it is not necessarily useful. We structure it in a way that I am sure some time in our past was useful, but that it doesn't work any more. We are trying to move toward the future with tools that not only are obsolete, but useless. We use an antique model we are hoping will take us someplace in this modern world. We try to use every second in the morning to sleep, but we waste hours before we go to bed. We run, get stressed and hurry in the morning, but waste hours that would have been useful the night before. We try to work after past midnight, when we are tired, only so that the next day we can barely think clearly. In case of any doubt, I am guilty of all these charges that are here claimed. I have done this many times and for many years. It was normal and I had seen many people do it too, like me, also for many years.

For some reason we have bought this idea of "normal". In fact, for many years I had joked that I am searching for a copy of the "Book of Normal" to see if I could understand so many normal things that, for me, made no sense at all. Of course, the fact that you discover that certain things make no sense at all doesn't mean you can do anything about it. Sometimes, even when you understand that something is absurd, you don't know how you could do it differently than the "normal" way; other times because this is the "normal" of some other person—in general someone close: your parents, wife or even our kids. Well, in this case that's exactly what I found in my life.

I am sure that this is somewhere on the famous "Book of Normal". You know down to the chapter of how to begin your day.

The fact is that even if our parents did this; our grandparents did it too, and even the parents and grandparents of our friends. They all ran around in the morning, races the tic-tock of the clock, that almost never won, left the house totally stressed out and tired to work. Those who didn't leave to work that way were, simply put, weird people. (and in many cases marked for the society because they didn't follow the rules established on the "Book of Normal".) Once they got to work, they began another race against the other clock—a race they hoped to win, but somehow lost every day. From there, exhausted, defeated, they try to have a personal life. We get home and begin the last count, the time to get to bed, and finally we lay in front of the television or a book. The next morning, we begin the race again, with the illusion that this time we are going to win. The "Book of Normal" apparently established that even though we are going to lose again, we need to believe that some day we may win. Even if that day never arrives.

We had lose this race for years and many would lose it for the rest of their lives, but what if there was a way to win it? I know that winning is not "normal", but what if there was a way to win it?

The only way to win this, in my experience, is to play with by different set of rules. Since I have been unable to find the "Book of Normal", I decided to defy it and create a new "normal", my own. One that I hope that it is not as "normal" but that allows me to win more often at the game of life.

We tend to put ourselves last in the race against time and hope that somehow we can win. Each time, we feel that we are farther from the mystic finish line. In many cases we have forgotten where the finish line is, we simply move like automations and hope that some day we will cross it. That it is one way to do it, I guess.

If you don't know where are you going, you are never going to get there. How do you know which step to take if you have no clue where are you going? Honestly, when you don't know, everything can be equally good or equally bad.

What I propose here is break the current existing structures, the normal thing, with its mystic book that no one knows (or at least that no one has ever show me) and begin to do things differently so it produces the results that we dream of—that ones that we yearn to someday reach.

Imagine that instead of doing the daily routine that failed you, you began your day three hours earlier and spent the first two doing those things that are important for you—not at the end of the day when you have no energy, but at the beginning when you are rested, with an ability to maximize your focus.

As I said previously, I know many people that it are going to use the argument that they are nocturnal people—I was also one. Many others are going to say that they can wake up at that time. I was unable to. Many are not going to be able to think during the first hours of the day, so why to be awake then? I used to say the same, until the brain and my body got used to the new schedule.

I am not saying it is the only way to do it, I am saying that it is a different way to do it—one that, in many cases, makes more sense.

The reality is that most people sleep fewer hours than they need and should; most people are simply exhausted. We continue trying to do those things that are important for us at midnight. For some reason, we don't contemplate waking up earlier, with more energy, and doing that thing that we consider the most important first. Instead we continue working hard; we try to be productive so we can get home earlier to do those important things. We hope that after a whole day, tired, we are going to have the energy, creativity and mental ability to think about those important things. Instead we sit, sleeping and in front of the television, and try to do that important thing for one more hour... until we collapse.

The reason to be productive isn't only that to accomplish the stuff that it is important for us; otherwise, why we want to be productive? Being productive just to be productive is simply absurd. Now, assuming that we are trying to be productive to be able to do those things that are important for us, then we have the same goal.

Many years ago I stop believing in the division between work and my personal life, and understood that there were simply things to do and priorities that crash against each other. It isn't that our workplaces don't want you to have a balanced life; it's that their priorities are different than yours, and this hope that these are going to change may be as hard as finding the first edition of the "Book of Normal". It isn't a balance problem; is a priority problem.

The problem of productivity is something new; for many years the norm was doing it on the other way. The Industrial Revolution is closer than what we think, and therefore the systems for manage your personal and working life are even more recent. For many, life and work for were simply different things for years. Now we all need to manage not only our working life but also our personal one; honestly this is something new. Some years ago one went to work and managed his or her working life and the personal finances. The person that stayed at home, was in charge of the personal life. Today, there isn't such distinction; it's as important to learn to manage your personal life as your professional one, and the two lives can no longer be considered different things. So it isn't about finding a balance between two things that doesn't exist; it's finding balance between the different priorities that hunt us daily.

Let's stop here for a second and think about the following. We wake up at 6:00 A.M. and begin a race against the clock to get to the office and work until 6:00 P.M. to get back home to take care of all of our stuff and our own responsibilities. Once all these are done, we have crumbs of energy left, and begin to do what it is important for ourselves. It is at that moment that finally you get silence. How many times you had bring work to home, thinking about work that night. We all need time to be in silence to think. Sometimes is that silence is what we need to fix a problem at work. Sometimes, buying a book is the best thing we can do at 2:00 P.M. If the plan is to wait until every responsibility is done, in general we are leaving the most important task for when we have less energy. According to the rumors, that was established in the "Book of Normal"

Now let's see... What will happen if you wake up at 4:00 A.M. and spend from 4:00 A.M to 6:00 A.M doing the task with the most impact, the most important? What would happen if instead of using crumbs of energy, you would use your highest energy level?

In my experience you will experience what you imagine. That is exactly what will happen. The difference for me, was simply incredible. I began to finish high impact tasks, things that in general took hours, in less than an hour. I began to study and understand things that I simply was lacking the time to do. For the first time in years I had fewer tasks, my list were getting shorter and I was seeing new stuff on them. My task list begin smelling like hope instead of like naphthalene.

If I would have read this before experiencing it, most likely would had thought what many will think: that I am absolutely crazy. In a certain way, I am. In another way, I have discovered in a world that has lost its focus, concentration, silence and the ability to work on my dreams a way to begin to focus, concentrate, work on silence, on my dreams and goals. Crazy? Maybe. Productive? Without any doubt.

I did this experiment to improve my productivity—to recover my ability to focus, my ability to accomplish those things that are important for me that were challenging by the constant noise in my head. Now I know, that at 4:00 A.M. I can accomplish a level of productivity, concentration and focus that most people don't know are possible on modern times.

Like any idea in productivity, the only way to know if this works is to test it. In my experience the result had been incredible. Honestly, had allowed me put what I have always considered important first and not the last as I did in the past. It may not fit everyone, it may not fit you, but those nights when I complaint at 9:00 P.M.—that I'm exhausted and ready to go to bed—the next morning at 7:00 A.M. I'm reminded of why this is a great idea. In general those three hours in the morning confirm to me, that I am doing it right.

SPECIAL THANKS

To my wife, my daughter and my son, who are simply amazing. I will never get tired of saying that.

To Isabel Pinaud, my sister and the one that design the amazing cover this book had.

To Kenn Rudolph, not only my friend but who also created the incredible covers of my other books and was willing to teach my sister for this one.

To those who always believed in me and who now smile when learning that I am a writer.

To those kind and generous eyes that read this when looked like a minefield, full of spelling and grammar errors.

To my parents, friends and family.

To all those who took the time to read this or any of my books.

To those who had given their reviews on this book or any other of my books.

To those people who in some way or another have helped me make this a reality.

ABOUT THE AUTHOR

I am a writer, a BestSeller Author in the US, UK, Germany, Spain and France. In another life I was a Lawyer in recovery and a former Technology Consultant and Salesman. My Passion is to Write. I have studied productivity and helping people with their productivity for the last ten years.

I am living in Fort Wayne, Indiana. I am married and have a little girl, a boy and two dogs who keep me in company. I spend my day teaching my daughter and son things, writing and washing dishes, because I believe in what Agatha Christie once said: "The best time for planning a book is while you're doing the dishes."My blog: www.augustopinaud.com

Twitter: apinaud

Email: augusto@augustopinaud.com

Facebook: http://www.facebook.com/augustopinaud/

Web Page of the Book:

http://www.4amAProductivityArgument.augustopinaud/

==